Morally Ambiguous

Ted Lavender

BookLeaf Publishing

India | USA | UK

Made with ❤ on the BookLeaf Publishing Platform
www.bookleafpub.in
www.bookleafpub.com

Dedication

to mom, i told you the first one published is yours
its a butful tesuday moring <3

Preface

"Morally Ambiguous" was born out of big feelings and a writing class that taught that poetry was whatever you made it to be. These poems are a reflection of the beauty hidden in the world, the ever changing life we live, the what could have been's of romance, and a fierce dedication to reality as reality is. As you journey through these poems, may you find solace and hope, love and loss, and an expectation of truth as you see fit. This collection is a celebration of the bond between the human nature and the human brain, a bond that nurtures us and reminds us to be true to who we are.

Acknowledgements

To my friend Ashlyn for her continuous support and determination to remind me that art speaks for the artist.
To the Campbell County Public Library for its unwavering commitment to provide free WiFi and computers to the public.
To Alex McIntosh for opening my eyes to the world of poetry and teaching me that poetry is whatever you make it.

Neuroses

These are the first stages of neurosis.
Compulsive acts to rearrange a content space. Manic pixie dream parades trotting along the walls. Stolen comic books from the local gas station growing piles in the corner.

These are the second stages of neurosis.
An unhealthy obsession of Randall from Monsters Inc. Playing music only on a phonograph console stereo and it's MARINA. Watching YouTubers play the Sims4. Coffee is no longer bought in shops, it's made in K-cups.

These are the third stages of neurosis.
Drinking Danimals with or without a straw. Creating a controlled chaos induced environment. Using a weekly pill tracker. Task and Hobby jumping. Taking public transit. Buying spray paint cans that end up as decoration. Getting grounded from Harry Potter. Shrek is your favorite meme.

This is the fourth stage of neurosis.
looking in the mirror
with no knowledge
of how to be better

the beginning

you can dance in a million stars
and ugly cry obscene storms
or run on the high of life
as long as you
 feel
we swim drunk
dance stars to
first tastes of
existing. whether
vibrant spring or
uncanny tomorrows
we *feel*
 life

moon's desire

the stars shine
bright
to illuminate the
moon
gazing at her
beauty
like clair de
lune

how it feels

sitting here feels
like the idea of
a cowboy

the lights
the stars
the burning desire
the passage of time

lonesome and stoic
backbreaking work
sweating in the sun
roasting beans over the fire

sleeping under the sky
thoughts of wonder and
heartbreak
gutters look at the stars too

Wonderment

What would it be like
to share a meal
on different plates?

One, a fine China with a matching tea cup and tray.
The other, a Spider-Man ramen bowl and a vintage Coca-
Cola glass.

Two hearts in tandem
different yet
aroused.
Boiling down to
similar disinterests.

Perhaps a shared spot on the couch
watching a new movie on an old VHS.
Huddled close together
for warmth, we would say.

The golden flame of your hair would be a
comfortable pillow.
My shoulder a sturdy headrest, just how
you like it.

i wonder
Would You Like It

what curiousness

what a fanatically odd,
beautiful world
to lie face down in

the dark grass
with luxurious problems
and delightful chaos.

what a crazy mad,
beguiling world
to wander between

the nuances of
an empty garden
or radiant purge

what a wildly complex,
puerile world
to boast an early

belief in love
that begins again
and again and

The Carnival

If I had a prize for every starlet I found in you,
I would be the worlds biggest carnival

Parading love across grass like funnel cake powder
Boasting cheers of happiness like screams on a tilt-a-
whirl
Creating memories that last for years and years

Your ticket would be free, Dear
You'd never have to pay

memories

i love the story
when you told it
but i
don't remember how it went

grounding in the spirit of
how it sounds
muscle memory tells me
i'm on the right track

so much depends upon
the essence of the tale

beginning to believe
i'll never get it back
too much fog that
refuses to lift

battling the memory with
a pencil as my
only line of defense
fluid with panic

knowing that
you'll never tell the story again

Anonymity

dried fruit
or
sky food
for those
     Yesterday Addicts
the fear of
submission
to the taste of
forever
     the Ones who Made it
new life on
top
same friends from
before
     The Newcomer
is the most
important
to come through
the door

The Head Piece

quick learning
"gets you far"

floating virtues
too close to the sun

the message being
do what you wish
get done onto you

pieces missing
unsure where to look

fires cascading
mind melting behavior

beautiful under love,
does grass
turn
to forest

written by

scavenged ink
and torn up notebooks,
an idea from the stars
kissed by the moon,
well-wishes of ancestors and
diseases passed down,
zero broken bones
or feats unable to be reached,
a taste for classical music
accompanied by earl grey,
fierce competition laced with
an unending hunger for more,
drunk nicotine regrets paired
night long dance benders,
unhealthy doses of self-reflection
by hour long bus rides,
tarot card readings under
stacks of unread books,
rain pouring down when
the sun is still shining,
sounds of gravel
under car tires,
the smell of flowers
beside the produce section,

wind chimes and
eucalyptus in the shower,
haughty ideals mixed with
periodical substitutions,
late night cheese snacks
hidden in the kitchen,
rewinding VHS tapes on
a tiny retro television,
triple loads of laundry out
of two laundry baskets,
tattoos and piercings
attempted by friends,
chickpea salads stolen and
created by dad,
mismatched silverware
shoved in a drawer,
magazine clippings strewn
across the floor,
curiously stretched out
to fit in this body.

the enemy of self

if not Thy Enemy
    she says
why ask for deception?
hold those twelve memories
like virtue with her
teeth that remember
companion long past.

If Not thy enemy
    she says
why fight against
the final thought?
stay true to that of
windows in house, a
conscious space to watch

If Not Thy Enemy
    she says
then place it softly.
fleshed out
and terrified,
the artist shall create
the obscenities of living

home

What if I came home to you
and the sun was shining through the windows
and the house smelled like fresh baked dough
and the dryer was running blankets to warm us up for
movie night
and the cat lazed about, reminding us to take it easy
and the couch had two spots, labelled by our butts
and the snacks were fulfilling and kind to our bodies
and the pressure of the day melted away
and the evening was full of laughter and chatter
and the drinks were light and sparkling
and the windows were open, letting in a cool draft
and the day blossomed slowly into night
and the bed swallowed us up when we finally retired
what if I came home to You

the world kept turning. i never forgave it for that

the day i lost my grandmother
i was in school
she was a thousand miles away
with barely a trace of life left
yet i still called her
told her i loved her
and that the phone calls we shared
would never cease in my memory

the day i lost my grandfather
i stood over his casket
in an empty room
afraid to touch his made up body
fearing that which was no longer there
i was his, just as he was mine
and for a few brief seconds,
i understood what that truly meant

the day i lost my childhood dog
i drove two hours home
to see the sunken form of a beefy young pup
who wasn't so young anymore
she clung to life to wait for me

the long wait outside the vet was almost a goodbye
i carried her inside
her ashes sit on the highest shelf in my closet

New Ideas

They say not to run from your problems
But who am I if not a skilled marathon runner
    the part of me hoping it's true
    next busses
    new dresses
Pacing at distances greater than before,
Outrunning my last stint
    the part of me hoping it stays the same
    phone calls
    quick smiles
Trekking cross country and breaking in new shoes
I'll call it "chasing my dreams"
    the part of me hoping all of it changes
    loneliness among friends
    driving past memories
And maybe my therapist
Won't be able to dissect the meaning

in contact with my skin

bare chested and alone
collected and homegrown
or is it

homegrown and collected?
something about being unelected
to provide for the ones you love

feeling forced to keep it in
but having deep urges to share
i should write in my journal more

but i don't want to bare
the consequences or the feet of my
unknowing-ness

the messy or the unbridled
the somethings i am not
but aren't i what it say-ess

aren't i the stranger on the pages that sits
so collectively in the words bore by
the ink or the lead

aren't i the dread that pours limitless amounts
of anguish and fear
that things are changing

that i too have grown into a person
of which i don't know anythaing
how silly a thought

how poor a rhyme

can you bear it

there's a life being lived that no longer pertains to you
-that no longer checks in
--tells you what that bitch at the coffee shop said to the
poor barista at 6:30am
---what milk it buys from the store
----the hyper-fixation it's currently on
-----food it gets at the new mom and pop diner that
opened two months ago that is a regular spot now
------how work did or didn't go
-------who said what when the drama went down and
everyone got pissy and butt-hurt at each other
--------why a new way to work was taken, just because
and also the traffic the normal way was backed up more
than usual
---------a rearrangement of the nightstand because
everything was getting cluttered and felt too stuffy next
to the bed
----------a decision to take a spontaneous trip to the next
town over to the best locally owned bookstore that has a
sale going on right now
-----------a casual walk to the bakery for a fresh
cinnamon raisin bagel, toasted with strawberry cream
smear and, maybe, a small caramel macchiato to go
------------the new plant bought, regretfully, at the

capitalistic supermarket because it was too darn cute to
leave wilting in that gross place

and maybe
you aren't supposed to know

let not

let not these empty
hands stab at wounds
too ossified to heal

let not these empty
ideas begin to blossom
against currents too substantial

let not these empty
plans turn to atrophy
to time lost abroad

let not these empty
hearts feel intimacy for
their commiseration fanes disdain

let not these empty
heads scheme pertinent speculations
against those that flourish

let not these empty
eyes wilt fabrications exposing
pains of their eminence

let not these empty
souls move gradually towards
desolate certifications of living

burning for company

company before breakfast
and he asks
if you can make eggs

you're on a random fast
you tell him
and he pairs an eye roll with a grimace

he's a first rate character
the voice says
no wonder you came so quickly

Banquets

Let the dogs go feral and the cats be mad
Let the acts of pilferage be enough to settle debts
Make the tides rise higher than timeshare expenditures
Make the Running of the Bulls stand for Digressions of
Man
Turn the faucet to boiling and watch creatures screech
death
Turn engagements of celebutante to a summons of
Bohemia
Forge christenings of subsumption that gape in
phenomena
Forge severance that fracture confines theorized resilient
Launch systems which starve media direction of
consciousness
Launch periods of contemplations against instructed
decorum
Bring accomplished appetites to trade percipience for a
menu
Bring art to a forefront that eradicate the reluctant
Take that which is yours,
    a vigor of unease

compulsive punctuality

<pre>
      a need to be   ~   there for her
       on time   ~   to calm the unrest
    knowing that a change ~   brought on by
        an unruly   ~   distraction of a
       self diagnosis ~   weeping displeasure
       can make   ~   forgetting the simplest
    facts feel like failure.   ~   ways of living
      begin to believe   ~   that a turning point
     in transformation ~   of doing the right thing
   to become someone who   ~ makes a person see that
          is enough   ~   for love
</pre>

*authors note: this is a contrapuntal poem, to be read as two separate poems or both together, the "~" is the indicator for separation between the two